I0128974

Islamism, Political Islam, and the Need for Critique

Paul Cliteur

Title: Islamism, Political Islam, and the Need for Critique

ISBN: 978-1-63902-934-1

Author: Paul Cliteur

Cover image: www.pixabay.com

Publisher: Generis Publishing
Online orders: www.generis-publishing.com
Contact email: info@generis-publishing.com

Table of Contents

Books by Paul Cliteur

Conservatisme en cultuurrecht (1989)

Humanistische filosofie (1990)

Filosofen van het hedendaags liberalisme, red. (1990)

Inleiding in het recht (1990)

Constitutionele toetsing (1991)

Geschiedenis van het humanisme, red. (1991)

Filosofen van het klassieke liberalisme, red. (1993)

Overtuigend bewijs, red. (1994)

Onze verhouding tot de apen (1995)

De filosofie van mensenrechten (1997)

Sociale cohesie en het recht, red. (1998)

Darwin, dier en recht (2001)

Moderne Papoea's (2002)

Rechten, plichten, deugden, red. (2003)

Encyclopedie van de rechtswetenschap, red. (2003)

Naar een Europese Grondwet, red. (2004)

Tegen de decadentie (2004)

Encyclopedie van de rechtswetenschap I, coauteur (2006)

Moreel Esperanto (2007)

Preambules, coauteur (2009)

Esperanto Moral (Spanish, 2009)

The Secular Outlook (2010)

Het monotheïstisch dilemma (2010)

In gesprek met Paul Cliteur, coauteur (2012)

La visione laica del mondo (Italian, 2013)

Het Atheïstisch Woordenboek, coauteur (2015)

The Fall and Rise of Blasphemy Law, red. (2016)

Legaliteit en legitimiteit, coauteur (2016)

Bardot, Fallaci, Houellebecq en Wilders (2016)

Mag God nog, coauteur (2017)

Constitutional Preambles, coauteur (2017)

Cultuurmarxisme, red. (2018)

In naam van God, coauteur (2018)

Moord op Spinoza, red. (2018)

Populist and Islamist Challenges for International Law, coauteur (2019)

A New Introduction to Jurisprudence (2019)

Diversiteit, identiteit en de 'culture wars', red. (2019)

Theoterrorism versus Freedom of Speech (2019)

Westerse schuld, red. (2021)

A New Introduction to Legal Method (2022)

Foreword

One of the remarkable differences between Western countries and Central European countries is that people in the West have proven to be highly vulnerable to jihadist terrorism. It cannot have escaped anyone's attention, but England, Germany, France, and the Netherlands have a "terrorism problem." In recent years, groups of young people have been receptive to the lure of jihad, and many left for Syria to fight for the caliphate there.

The corona pandemic has pushed the focus on jihadist terrorism into the background, but that will only be temporary. France, in particular, is a country heavily hit by jihadist attacks. It is now involved in a significant public debate about what explains the failure to prevent the attacks.

Ironically, the crude jihadist violence is often in response to Islam-critical cartoons. Immediately after the murder of Theo van Gogh in the Netherlands (2004), people in Denmark wanted to test whether it was possible to make critical cartoons about the Islamic prophet Mohammed. This led to the Danish Cartoon Affair (2005). Exactly ten years later, the murder of virtually the entire editorial staff of the satirical weekly *Charlie Hebdo* (2015) put an end to satire that jihadists do not appreciate and vowed to avenge. Another five years later, in 2020, French teacher Samuel Paty was beheaded because he had shown in his social studies classes one of the cartoons that had sparked the controversy.

All of this means that Western European countries are failing to live up to one of the fundamental aspirations of their founding texts: guaranteeing freedom of thought, conscience, and religion, especially the freedom to change religion and criticize religion.

Here's how it works. Religion gets protection in law. In 1948, the United Nations launched the Universal Declaration of Human Rights. Article 18 declares:

> Everyone has the right to freedom of thought, conscience and religion; this right includes freedom to change his religion or belief, and freedom, either alone or in community with others and in public or private, to manifest his religion or belief in teaching, practice, worship and observance.

This 1948 provision, then only a declaration of intent, was later enshrined in real, legally binding documents, for example, in the European Convention for the Protection of Human Rights and Fundamental Freedoms (1950), better known as the European Convention on Human Rights.

The European Convention on Human Rights includes Article 9. This article has two sections, and both are relevant to protecting religious freedom. The first section reads as follows:

> Everyone has the right to freedom of thought, conscience and religion; this right includes freedom to change his religion or belief, and freedom, either alone or in community with others and in public or private, to manifest his religion or belief, in worship, teaching, practice and observance.

One of the most essential parts of that text is the freedom to change religion or belief.

What makes this so unique? That is, one has the freedom to choose a religion but also to leave a religion. What are the consequences of that? Does this mean that the European Convention on Human Rights also recognizes a right to abandon one's faith? That is, to exchange theism for atheism?

The European Court in Strasbourg that is is the judicial authority on the interpretation of the Convention answered this vital question in 1993, in the case of *Kokkinakis v. Greece*. The Kokkinakis case was named after the Greek evangelist Minos Kokkinakis (1909-1999). Kokkinakis was a Greek member of Jehovah's Witnesses. Kokkinakis gained notoriety for his repeated clashes with the Greek ban on proselytism. Like the first apostles, Kokkinakis was from a simple background. He was a shopkeeper by profession. Initially, he was a member of the Greek Orthodox Church, but in 1936 he switched to the Church of the Jehovah's Witnesses. Kokkinakis thus practiced the freedom for which Art. 9 ECHR provides the basis: the freedom to change one's religion.

Kokkinakis came into conflict with the Greek government. Not because of his apostasy from the Greek Orthodox Church, but because of his intrusive evangelizing, a form of action known as proselytizing.

Crucially, in the case of Kokkinakis v. Greece, the ECtHR took a position on how we should view the freedom to change one's religion. Does this include the freedom to become an atheist? The ECtHR answers that question with an unconditional "yes." Here we find the passage in which the ECtHR takes a position on this question: "As laid down in Article 9 (art. 9), freedom of thought, conscience and religion is one of the foundations of a 'democratic society' within the meaning of the Convention. It is, in its religious dimension, one of the most vital elements that make up the identity of believers and their conception of life, but it is also a precious commodity for atheists, agnostics, skeptics and the unchurched. The pluralism that is inseparable from a democratic society and that has been fought for dearly over the centuries depends on it" (*Kokkinakis*, para. 31).

This is essential information. Art. 9 ECHR protects not only the interests and rights of believers who wish to change from one religious position to another religious position (e.g., apostasy from Greek Orthodox to Jehovah's Witness) but also the change from a religious position to a non-religious position. Three categories of stakeholders are then explicitly mentioned by the ECtHR:

1. Atheists,
2. Agnostics,
3. Skeptics, and
4. The unconcerned.

This worldview of atheists, agnostics, skeptics, and the unconcerned clashes heavily with the theocentric and theocratic ambitions of jihadi terrorism. The last has vowed to counter secular satire and parody and to destroy the symbolic agents of Western liberalism. And in this, they are pretty successful. Western countries generally respond to their violence by ignoring it. *Islamism, Political Islam, and the Need for Critique* tries to analyse the challenges we face and what we can do about them.

Abstract

This article is about Islamism (or political Islam) as a challenge for contemporary liberal democracies. Islamism is portrayed as an ideology that favors one specific religion as supreme and that is a threat to freedom of speech. The author makes a plea for distinguishing a. the religion of Islam, b. Muslims as a group, and c. the political ideology of Islamism. Regarding the dangers of Islamism, some sociological research about the convictions of Muslims is discussed (Koopmans, Esposito) and the most recent case from the European Court of Human Rights in Strasbourg (*E.S. v. Austria* (2018)) is analysed which, basically, means that all criticism of Islam and Islamism difficult, if not impossible.

Keywords. Islamism. Religious terrorism. Theoterrorism. Freedom of Speech. Religious criticism. Islamophobia. Elisabeth Sabaditsch-Wolff. E.S. v. Austria (ECHR). Koopmans. Esposito.

Islamism as a challenge for liberal democracies

After Communism and Nazism, nowadays, Islamism poses a challenge for liberal democracies. Not only in the West, but everywhere in the world. Islamism is an 'ism'. That is, it is an ideology like anarchism, communism, liberalism, socialism, Nazism, and fascism. The suffix 'ism' makes clear that Islamism does not primarily *describe* reality but has a normative goal (it is 'prescriptive').

Compare Islamism with other ideologies. Liberalism tries to realize 'liberty' in the world. Communism is motivated by an idea of 'community'. Nazism wants to achieve a world where 'race' is the ultimate point of reference. Islamism makes religion, one religion in fact, the focus of its attention: Islam. Islam is not seen as just a religion, as merely a spiritual guide for the individual, but as a comprehensive doctrine guiding the individual, the community, and the state. And this down to the smallest details. [I am much indebted to Pierre-André Taguieff's *L'islamisme et nous* (2017).]

As Megnad Desai writes in *Rethinking Islamism* (2007: preface), this is not without consequences. Islamism is an ideology whose nature has to be grasped if, e.g., we are to fight terrorism.

Let me first present some definitions before I elaborate on this point because this will give us conceptual clarity. Some scholars use a word other than 'Islamism' to describe the ideological threat. 'Islamism' (Cliteur, 2011: pp. 154–67; Cox and Marks, 2011; Meghnad, 2007; Tibi, 2012) is used interchangeably with the terms 'political Islam' (Tibi, 2008; Hirsi Ali, 2017; Ellian, 2008: pp. 87–102; Kepel, 2004), 'radical Islam' (Dutch General Intelligence and Security Service, 2004; Bawer, 2006; Burke, 2003: pp. 72–73; Gabriel, 2008; Husain, 2007; Marshall, 2005), and 'Islamic fundamentalism' (Euben, 1997: pp. 28–55; Jansen, 1997; Najjar, 1998: pp. 139–168; Zee, 2015). Karima Bennoune, author of *Your Fatwa Does Not Apply Here: Untold Stories from the Fight against Muslim Fundamentalism* (2013), prefers the term 'Muslim fundamentalism' to 'Islamism'. She considers the term 'fundamentalist' more accurate than 'Islamist' because the last word is potentially derogatory to Islam itself and privileges 'Islamist' claims of authenticity (Bennoune, 2009; pp. 635–198; Bennoune, 2002: pp. 75–91; *see also* Ramadani, 2017: p. 191). Martha Minow, in contrast, speaks of

'Islamism' in "Tolerance in an Age of Terror" (2007: pp. 453–94, pp. 462, 476, 479).

Other scholars describe 'Islamism' as 'political Islam'. The German feminist author Alice Schwarzer, one of the rare feminist authors addressing this topic, speaks of 'Islamism' as something 'political' in contrast to Islam as a 'religion'. Islamists use Islam as a political strategy, she says (2010: p. 14). And Guy Haarscher writes that 9/11 revealed 'the new adversary' of our time: 'radical Islamist terrorism' ([1993] 2015: p. 9). The Algerian novelist Boualem Sansal describes the rise of Islamism in the Arab world as a political ambition to 'rule in the name of Allah' (2013).

An important question is how to define 'political Islam'. The German philosopher Michael Schmidt-Salomon writes that political Islam (or Islamism) is a political movement that aims to organize state and society based on Islamic principles. Those Islamic principles are based on a particular way of interpreting the Koran, the hadith, and the Islamic tradition of law (sharia) (2016: p. 56). 'Political Islam rejects any kind of distinction between religion and politics, mosque and state. Political Islam even rejects the modern state in favor of a caliphate' (Hirsi Ali, 2017: p. 10). Terri Murray supports this view in *Identity Islam and the Twilight of Liberal Values*

(2018) when she writes: 'Islamists' ultimate aim is a global caliphate'.

There seems to be a growing group of scholars that makes use of the distinction between Islam and Islamism (or political Islam). Bassam Tibi, in *Islamism and Islam* (2012), describes Islamism as a political ideology based on a reinvented version of Islamic law. Caroline Cox and John Marks in *The West, Islam and Islamism* (2003: p. 6) use the term 'Islamism' to refer to a radical, militantly ideological version of Islam, as interpreted by practitioners, in which violent actions such as terrorism, suicide bombings, or revolutions are explicitly advocated, practiced, and justified using religious terminology. Pierre-André Taguieff, in his book *L'islamisme et nous* (2017) presents many authors and books that take the concept of Islamism as their point of departure.

A comprehensive doctrine

Islamism is an 'ism' in the sense that it has a goal, a political ideal, and a worldview that it wants to realize in this world. What is that goal?

As indicated, the aim of Islamism is to make Islam the ultimate frame of reference not only for individual lives but also for the state, for politics, for everything. The aim of Islamism is to grant one specific religion a position religions are never supposed to have in a democracy: above the law as the legitimate expression of the will of the people, above the state as the organization people have chosen to administer their daily affairs, above everything else. One of the most important political goals for Islamists is to organize an Islamic state, based on Islamic holy law: sharia (Tibi, 2013; Zee, 2014: pp. 1–18; Zee, 2015).

According to Islamism, Islam is not a 'religion' in the sense of a spiritual option for the individual; instead, it is what John Rawls would call a 'comprehensive doctrine': an all-enveloping perspective one must live by. It is therefore not surprising, as Tarek Osman writes in *Islamism* (2016: p. ix), that secularists and Islamists are engaged in a protracted fight about cultural hegemony in the Middle East and also in other parts of the world where Islam is an significant factor. Secularism is the exact antithesis of Islamism and vice versa. Islamists want to fuse religion and politics as much as possible; secularists want to separate those two domains (Zuckerman and Shook, 2017). Feminist author Alice Schwarzer calls Islamism 'the political instrumentalization of faith' (2010: p. 28). Sharia is particularly harmful to women's rights, as the Dutch scholar Machteld Zee has made clear in her research into British Sharia Councils (2015; 2014: pp. 1–18). Susan Moller Okin criticized 'multiculturalism' because it so often condones practices that are harmful to women's rights (1999).

Why Islamism is not talked about

For a long time, it was not very common for a politician to comment on the motives of terrorists. They were characterized as 'monsters' or 'criminals', but politicians were keen to avoid all further comments on the worldview of the terrorists themselves. Some politicians did not heed this taboo, but the majority did.

After the London Bridge attack in June 2017, British Prime Minister Theresa May, leader of the British conservatives, entangled in a ferocious debate about Britain's withdrawal from the European Union, made a change. She explicitly referred to the ideological background of the terrorists. These 'recent attacks', she said, 'are bound together by the single evil ideology of Islamist extremism that preaches hatred, sows division and promotes sectarianism' (Samuelson, 2017). From the perspective of left-wing liberals such as Madeleine Albright, such a statement may nurture 'a paranoid bigotry towards the followers of one of the world's foremost religions' (2018: p. 5). Of course, May does not speak of Islam but of Islamism. But that does not make her any more acceptable from the perspective of certain modern 'anti-fascists'. May, like Desai, like Bennoune, like Schwarzer, like Sansal, constructs a relationship between terrorist acts and a religion that is a minority religion in the Western world. And Muslims, as a minority, have the status of vulnerable citizens. Thus, certain progressive left-wing movements automatically assume the role of protectors of those vulnerable minorities simply because they are minorities. The old proletariat is no longer interesting for them, but the 'minorities' are. The mirror image of this new role the Left has constructed for itself is that all those commentators who do not comply with the new language taboos are stigmatized as 'right wing' or 'populist'. So May is, in this sense, a 'populist' and 'right wing'. She is right wing because she does not observe the language taboos the Left has newly invented. [President Trump also gave a speech on terrorism while still a candidate (Trump, 2016), which he repeated in Saudi Arabia as president (*See* Trump, 2017). President Obama consistently refused to refer to the ideological background of the terrorist attacks (*See* Obama, 2009).]

May continued with some remarks about the content of that ideology: 'It is an ideology that claims our Western values of freedom, democracy and human rights are incompatible with the religion of Islam'.

The first remark is about the motivation of the attackers: this motivation is ideological. The second remark is about the content of the ideology, although only negatively defined: it is against freedom, democracy, and human rights. [Also, '[t]oo long emphasis was placed on the social-economic factors as a 'cause' of resurging jihadism and radicalization. The motto was: create jobs and jihadism will crumble'. (Pierik, 2015: p. 45).]

A third remark by the prime minister is about theology. She said, 'It is an ideology that is a perversion of Islam and a perversion of the truth'. And after that, she made a reference (although not using the concept by name) to what some authors have referred to as 'militant democracy' (Rijpkema, 2018). She said, 'Defeating this ideology is one of the great challenges of our time, but it cannot be defeated by military intervention alone. It will not be defeated by the maintenance of a permanent defensive counter-terrorism operation, however skillful its leaders and practitioners'. In other words, democracies ought to mobilize resistance against the ideologies that undermine democracy. Britain's prime minister recognizes that there is a spiritual challenge for contemporary democracies and that this has to be countered by some sort of cultural resistance. 'It will only be defeated when we turn people's minds away from this violence and make them understand that our values—pluralistic British values—are superior to anything offered by the preachers and supporters of hate'. [We find a similar approach to the topic of democracy from Speaker of the House of Representatives in the Netherlands Ms. Khadija Arib, who raises the question of what to do with a group that uses democracy and the rule of law to abolish democratic freedoms for others (2017).] [The father of the idea of 'Militant Democracy' is the Dutch constitutional scholar Van den Bergh (*See* Van den Bergh, 2019: pp. 367–391). The concept is also used by Karl Loewenstein (1937a: pp. 417–432; 1937b: pp. 638–658) and by András Sajó (2004a: pp. 231–245; 2004b: pp. 245–265).]

May's reference to the 'superiority' of the values of liberal democracy over those of Islamist extremism makes her an opponent of cultural relativism, which teaches that no set of values has superiority over any other (Gardner, 1996: pp. 149–61; Gensler, 1998: pp. 11–20). May seems to think that our present time demands a rejection of that relativism.

Important ideologues of Islamism

The founding fathers of Islamism are Hasan al-Banna (1906–49), Sayyid Qutb (1906–66), Abul Ala Maududi (1903–73), and the Iranian cleric and politician Ruhollah Khomeini (1902–89), leader of the 1979 Iranian Revolution.

Mentioning the last one, Khomeini, as one of the founding fathers of Islamism, could prompt the idea that Islamists are exclusively revolutionaries. This is not true (Schmidt-Salomon, 2016: pp. 40–42). Reformist Islamists can also work *within* the system by using the democratic process to come to power. The Tunisian Ennahda Movement and the Jamaat-e-Islami of Pakistan, for instance, are commonly mentioned as examples of democratic participation of Islamist groups. Also, Hezbollah in Lebanon and Hamas in Palestine participate in the democratic system. And further, the Egyptian Muslim Brotherhood, although one of the most vital Islamist movements, is not necessarily undemocratic in the sense of being opposed to majority vote, or revolutionary in the sense of being committed to the violent overthrow of a regime.

Chief sources of inspiration for Islamists in the more distant past are Ibn Taymiyyah and Muhammad ibn Abd-al-Wahhab. Ibn Taymiyyah (1263–1328) is a Syrian Islamic legal scholar from the 13th and 14th centuries. He exerted a prodigious influence on contemporary Islamists. Ibn Taymiyyah argued forcefully for the dominance of sharia law, and he was heavily opposed to all forms of syncretism (Christian influence on Islamic doctrine).

Another source of inspiration for contemporary Islamists is Muhammad ibn Abd-al-Wahhab (1703–92), a cleric from Arabia who advocated a return to a literal interpretation of the Koran and emulating the life of Mohammed. He was the founder of Wahhabism, which became the official variant of Islam in Saudi Arabia.

Contemporary authors on the conflict between Islamism and democracy

There is a discussion among scholars and, interestingly, also among nonscholars (in particular politicians) about whether this distinction between the religion of Islam and the ideology of Islamism makes any sense. There are Islam scholars who say this distinction is artificial, misleading, and even obfuscatory because Islam, as a religion, is all-enveloping, so any ideological distinction from Islamism is merely illusory. Some of the most well-known representatives of this direction are Martin Hartmann (1851–1918) in Germany (1910: pp. 72–92; 1909), Robert Spencer (*b.* 1962) in the United States (2015; 2012; 2002), and Anne-Marie Delcambre (1943–2016) in France (2003; 2004; 2006; 2009). But there are also scholars who think this distinction is essential and should be made. Representatives of the 'Islamism school' are Daniel Pipes (*b.* 1949) ([2002] 2005; 2002), Bassam Tibi (*b.* 1944) ([1998] 2001; 2012; 2013), Hamed Abdel-Samad (*b.* 1972) (2016; 2010; 2011; 2009; 2015), Maaijd Nawaz (*b.* 1977) (and Harris, 2015), Pierre-André Taguieff (*b.* 1946) (2017), Susanne Schröter (*b.* 1957) (2019), and Elham

Manea (*b.* 1966) (2018). [*See also* the authors represented in the book by Linnemann, Carsten, Bausback, et al. (2019).]

Sometimes, the Islamism school seeks to salvage what they see as an uncorrupted, pure Islam from historical accretions. Representatives sometimes also claim that every quest for some pure Islam is fruitless. Islam is simply what manifests itself in social reality as such.

Some of the members of the Islamism school make a Kantian bifurcation in reality between the 'Ding an sich' (true nature) and 'empirical manifestations' of Islam. The most rigorous Kantians do not pretend to make assertions about the nature of the 'Ding an sich'. The 'true nature' of the religion can never be ascertained. In the world of 'empirical manifestations' (*'Erscheinungen'*), we can only see what religion means to 'us' subjectively. Thus, more rigorous members of the Islamism school take an agnostic approach to Islam's true nature. But many adherents do not comply with this rigorous stance: they speculate about the 'thing in itself'. A clear example is the previous prime minister of the United Kingdom, Theresa May, who claims to 'know' that the Islamists have perverted the true nature of Islam: 'It is an ideology that is a perversion of Islam and a perversion of the truth', she stated confidently. Karen

Armstrong's *A History of God* ([1993] 1999) also contains a long parade of ideas about the 'true nature' of the religions she describes, unaffected by the mistaken interpretations of followers she dismisses as 'fundamentalists' or otherwise deluded. Thus, some members of the Islamism school select a certain innocuous manifestation of Islam as the true nature of Islam.

Madeleine Albright, who decried paranoia and bigotry toward 'the followers of one of the world's foremost religions' (2018: p. 5), is also in that category. Her remarks portray theological stances that she has insufficient knowledge to defend. It would be much more modest for politicians to say that they lack the scholarly expertise to make firm assertions about the nature of a world religion. But Albright thinks that *because* a religion is a world religion, this guarantees its moral respectability. This is strange. This elementary mistake would not be made about ideologies. If someone claimed that a comment criticizing an ideology was paranoid bigotry toward the followers of one of the world's foremost ideologies, and thereby argued that such beliefs should be immune from criticism, everyone would find this is a very strange way to immunize fascism, Nazism, or communism against critique. But when it comes to religions, people have the idea that the more influential they become, the more followers they have, the more morally correct they become.

Another reason that may explain the enormous animosity between especially radical representatives of the three monotheist creeds is presented by the Moroccan novelist Tahar Ben Jelloun. Ben Jelloun points out that the pretense of Jews, Christians, and Muslims is that they revere the same God ([2002] 2012: p. 38). Prima facie that could be a source of common understanding. But on further inspection, it can also function as a source of bitter conflict: the other does not revere another god but *your God,* about whom he or she has twisted opinions.

Instead, the 'agnostic' approach for politicians commenting on Islamism might be to say, 'I do not know enough about the nature of Islam, but what is most important is what I see. And I see that many radical and violent people find a source of inspiration in some interpretation of Islam. Whether the true nature of Islam is peace or war is not for me to decide, but I know that Islamism is problematic'. But this is not what many politicians do. They want to believe in a peaceful core of Islam, and what they wish for they proclaim as the actual nature of things.

A popular candidate for this innocuous Islam, this true, peaceful nature of Islam, is Sufism. Sufis teach that real Islam has to do not with law or sharia or jihad but with experience. As American scholar of religion Stephen Prothero writes, 'It is about the heart-and-soul connection between the individual believer and God' (2010: p. 57). Sufis do not want to die before they can experience the divine. They want to taste God in the here and now. Because every place is equally sacred, you do not need to travel to Mecca or to a mosque to find God. Listening to Karen Armstrong or Tony Blair (Cliteur, 2015: pp. 374–403) when they talk about 'religions', one might get the impression that the core of Islam is Sufism. But others deny this. What puts us on the track of a more sober reading of the nature of Islam is the story of the Muslim pirates as told by Ali Rizvi in his book *The Atheist Muslim* (2016).

The story of the Muslim pirates

In 1786, Thomas Jefferson, when he was ambassador to France, accompanied by Secretary of Foreign Affairs John Jay, inquired from what source the Muslim pirates derived their right to pillage American ships before the coast of North Africa, and he got a very straightforward answer from Tripoli's envoy to London, Sid Haji Abdul Rahman Adja:

The Ambassador answered us that it was founded on the Laws of the Prophet; that it was written in their Koran; that all nations who should not have acknowledged their authority were sinners; that it was their right and duty to make war upon them wherever they could be found; and to make slaves of all they could take as prisoners; and that every Musselman who should be slain in battle was sure to go to Paradise (quoted in Rizvi, 2016: p. 18).

Rizvi offers interesting commentary on this passage:

Obviously, this is before the Islamic State or Al Qaeda. It's before the creation of Israel or the Arab-Israeli conflict. It's before Ayatollah Khomeini and the Iranian revolution; before Saudi Arabia; before the Taliban; before drone strikes; before the Cold War or the World Wars; before Herzl founded the Zionist movement; before Americans knew what jihad or even Islam was; before the United States had ever engaged in any military operation overseas; and—importantly—well before the existence of any established U.S. foreign policy (2016: p. 18).

[Needless to say, this episode occurred at a time when the United States had not yet abolished slavery. Jefferson owned over 600 African-American slaves, although he seems to have wrestled with the issue (*See* Schwabach, 2010: pp. 1–60).]

I do not analyze and further comment on this discussion among scholars. Karen Armstrong, Theresa May, and Madeleine Albright will undoubtedly say the ambassador has a twisted notion of what the 'true nature' of Islam is. But for our purposes this is less important. We can seek to remain neutral, and that means 'agnostic'. We want to seek common ground by noticing that all participants in the discussion at least agree that (1) there is a political manifestation of Islam called Islamism, and (2) it presents considerable problems. So, the Islamism school in its 'agnostic' variant will guide us here (and not the 'gnostic' version of Armstrong, May, and other politicians that claim to know the true nature of Islam).

To avoid confusing discussions about the political manifestations of Islam, it may be useful to distinguish the following as distinct concepts:

1. The religion of Islam,
2. Muslims as a group, and
3. The political ideology of Islamism.

I will focus on 2 and 3. And that makes it necessary to focus on sociological research into the ideas which are prevalent in the Muslim community.

Sociological research

This type of sociological research has been conducted by, among others, the Dutch sociologist Ruud Koopmans, connected to the Berlin Humboldt University (Berlin Social Science Center). Koopmans and his team were interested in 'fundamentalist attitudes' among Muslims, and his research pointed out that there was a considerable amount of fundamentalism among Muslims in certain European countries: 'Islamic fundamentalism is widely spread' (2013).

Koopmans analyzed data from a representative survey among immigrants and natives in six European countries. Two-thirds of the Muslims interviewed say that religious rules are more significant to them than the laws of the state in which they live (2013).

It is interesting to compare these findings with figures from other religions. Only 13 percent of Christians put religious rules above national law. According to Koopmans, there is a powerful tendency toward Muslim religious fundamentalism. And this is alarming.

'Fundamentalism is not an innocent form of strict religiosity', he says. Almost 60 percent of the Muslim respondents reject homosexuals as friends. With Christians, this figure is significantly lower: 13 percent do not want to have homosexuals as friends. Among Muslims there is also a great mistrust of Jews: 45 percent think that Jews cannot be trusted. With Christians, again, this figure is considerably lower (2013).

That brings us back to a distinction made in the previous paragraphs about (1) the religion of Islam, (2) Muslims as a group, and (3) the political ideology of Islamism. On the basis of empirical research by Koopmans among Muslims as a group (the second point), we might say that the religion of Islam (the first point) is heavily tainted by convictions that we associate with the political ideology of Islamism (the third point). And that is relevant information for what we may call the 'Islamist challenge' for democracy (*see* Cliteur and Guiora, 2019).

Let us compare Koopmans's findings with older research conducted by people with a different background. In 2007, American Islam scholar John L. Esposito and Dalia Mogahed, a senior analyst and executive director of the Gallup Center for Muslims Studies, presented the results of one of the most elaborate studies into 'what Muslims think'. Esposito and Mogahed's book, *Who Speaks for Islam? What a Billion Muslims Really Think* (2007), comprises the results of a Gallup poll, interspersed with Esposito's commentary on those results. Presenting the results of their poll, Esposito and Mogahed write, 'In totality, we surveyed a sample representing more than 90% of the world's 1.3 billion Muslims, making this the largest, most comprehensive study of contemporary Muslims ever done' (p. xi). Esposito, like so many others, was also interested in the question of what support there was in the Muslim community for the use of violence. This is what they found:

According to the Gallup Poll, 7% of respondents think that the 9/11 attacks were 'completely' justified and view the United States unfavorably. Among those who believe that the 9/11 attacks were not justified, whom we'll call 'moderates', 40% are pro-United States, but 60% view the United States unfavorably (p. 70).

Esposito underscores the hope that we may entertain because 93 percent of Muslims are 'moderate'. Nevertheless, he also discloses what 7 percent of 1.3 billion means in actual numbers: 91 million. In other words, 91 million Muslims think that the attacks of 9/11 were 'completely justified'.

Whether this justifies hope and a certain amount of optimism or should be a matter of grave concern is something that divides commentators.

That brings me to the last topic I want to discuss in this article. Let me summarize our findings so far. I do not want to go into the 'true nature' of Islam but focus on the political manifestations of this religion (Islamism). These political manifestations give us cause for concern. Whether we take the Koopmans' sociological research as our point of departure or Esposito's makes no great difference. The figures are not comforting. Islamic culture, Islamic lore, and the convictions of Muslims need to be critically scrutinized, discussed, and reformed. At the same time, this is more difficult than ever. Religious terrorists ('theoterrorists') intimidate authors who engage in this type of activity. This is the lesson we should have learned from the Rushdie controversy (1989) or at least from the attack on *Charlie Hebdo* (2015) (Tibi, 2019a: pp. 342–351; Tibi, 2019b: p. 9; Hasan, 2012; Murray, 2018). And not only is there the physical threat from the side of terrorists, there is also the legal threat from governments, lawmakers, and courts, which make criticism of everything that has to do with Islam, the convictions of Muslims, and even Islamism ever more difficult. As the French author Pierre-André Taguieff writes: 'Concernant la critique de l'islam, le déclin de la liberté d'expression, en France comme ailleurs, est un fait bien établi' (2017: p. 116). This author makes another pertinent observation:

On a souvent relevé le paradoxe tragi-comique: plus le terrorisme islamiste tue en Occident, et plus l'on dénonce l'islamophobie des Occidentaux (*see* 2017: p. 116).

Taguieff is wrong, however, when he claims that this paradox has often been noted ('relevé'). The problem is, it is totally ignored. At least to my knowledge. This is not very strange because this fact is wholly counterfactual. One would expect that because religious terrorists ('theoterrorists') make the claim that they are religiously motivated, this would stimulate critical research into Islam and discussions on the results of this research. The contrary is true. The concept of 'islamophobia' is used to stifle any criticism and critical research into Islam (Hasan, 2019: pp. 13–20).

I will conclude this contribution with an example from the European Court of Human Rights in Strasbourg from 2018. It is, in my view, an excellent example of the process that Taguieff describes. This judgment makes critically discussing Islam, Islamic culture, and in particular the convictions of the Muslim community difficult, if not impossible. This is the case of the Austrian Elisabeth Sabaditisch-Wolff.

Elisabeth Sabaditsch-Wolff

Elisabeth Sabaditsch-Wolff was convicted for (1) 'denigration of religious beliefs of a legally recognized religion', which is sanctioned in Section 188 of the Austrian Criminal Code, and (2) incitement to hatred, penalized in Article 283 of the same code. The first article punishes the *Herabwürdigung religiöser Lehren*, the defamation of religious doctrines (*E.S. v. Austria*, 2018: para 3). Ms. Sabaditsch's conviction was based on what was said during a seminar, 'Basic Information on Islam' ('Grundlagen des Islams'). On October 15 and November 12, 2009, she hosted a seminar with around 30 participants at each gathering (para 8). But not only ordinary participants were present. 'One of the participants was an undercover journalist working for a weekly journal' (para 8). ['The applicant's statements were in fact recorded by a journalist, who had participated in the seminar, and whose employer subsequently reported them to the public prosecutor' (para 51).]

When Sabaditsch-Wolff was questioned by the police concerning 'certain statements' she had made during the seminars, it appeared that the journalist had requested a preliminary investigation of her (para 8). The Austrian court found that she was guilty of 'publicly disparaging an object of veneration of a domestic church or religious society, namely Muhammad, the Prophet of Islam, in a manner capable of arousing justified indignation' (*'geeignet, berechtigtes Ärgernis zu erregen'*) (para 12).

What had Sabaditsch-Wolff said about Mohammed that led to her conviction? She was convicted based on two criticisms, one general and one specific. The more general criticism was about her contesting the status of Mohammed as 'the ideal man', 'the perfect human' (para 13). She voiced three complaints: first, that Mohammed was a warlord; second, that Mohammed endorsed polygamy; and third, that 'he liked to do it with children'. For these reasons, he was not the most perfect man.

One may object, what does that matter? Why is this important to digress upon in *our time*, more than seven centuries beyond Mohammed's lifetime? Sabaditsch-Wolff's answer to that question was that moral commentary on the life of the Prophet is vital because contemporary Muslims see him as a model to emulate. So when today's Muslims get into conflicts with democracy and 'our system of values', Sabaditsch-Wolff said, we can understand these conflicts by examining the background of the moral icon they try to copy (para 13).

The second point that got Sabaditsch-Wolff into trouble was her more specific critique of the Prophet. For this, she had used one of the most central Hadith collections available, that of Muhammad al-Bukhari (810–70). This collection of hadiths has great authority in the Muslim world. If something is included in Al-Bukhari's collection, it has the status of holy scripture. In this collection, there is a story about Mohammed, a man of middle age at that point, and his wife Aisha. When Mohammed married Aisha, she was six years old (para 13), and the marriage was consummated when she was nine (para 14).

According to Sabaditsch-Wolff, this was a matter of great moral concern and had far-reaching consequences. During the seminar, she had discussed this by relating a conversation she had had with her sister on how to interpret this historical issue. During that conversation, she had asked her sister, 'A 56-year-old and a six-year-old? What do you call that? Give me an example? What do we call it, if it is not paedophilia?' (para 13) Her sister had said, 'Those were different times'. But Sabaditsch-Wolff had been adamant: 'It wasn't okay back then, and it's not okay today' (para 13).

Sabaditsch-Wolff also discussed the relevance of this story for our contemporary world: 'It is still happening today' (para 13). She means, child marriages are still organized in the Islamic world. The moral legitimacy of these marriages is found in a record considered historically uncontestable by at least some Muslims.

The Austrian Regional Court did not comment on whether *the story* was considered historically accurate in the Muslim world, nor did it discuss *the significance* of this story for the position of underaged girls in the Islamic world. The Court only commented on one aspect: Could Sabaditsch-Wolff's conversation with her sister be interpreted as conveying the message that Mohammed had 'paedophilic tendencies'? And if so, could this be considered 'publicly disparaging an object of veneration of a domestic church or religious society' (para 12)? The Court answered affirmatively because Sabaditsch-Wolff 'had suggested that Muhammed was not a worthy subject of worship' (para 12). The word 'paedophilia' was capable of 'arousing indignation', the Austrian Court said. A reason the Austrian Court considered the word 'paedophilia' inapplicable was that when Aisha had turned 18, the Prophet had not annulled the marriage (para 12).

Another point discussed before the Austrian Court was whether something said at a gathering of 30 people is sufficiently 'public' to warrant a conviction. The Austrian Court answered in the affirmative because 'it was conceivable that at least some of the participants might have been disturbed by the statements' (para 14).

But what about the point of Mohammed's exemplary role, the Prophet being an object of emulation? The Austrian Court ignored the issue and only said that Sabaditsch-Wolff's discussion did 'not contribute to a debate of public interest' (para 14). Her statements had not been 'statements of fact' but only 'derogatory value statements' (para 15). Discussing child marriages would have been possible, according to the Austrian Court, but this is not the same as pedophilia (para 15). Besides, child marriage is not only a 'phenomenon of Islam' but also among the European dynasties (para 15). The Austrian Court also scolded the applicant for her conception of (or rather lack of) tolerance. 'Presenting objects of religious worship in a provocative way capable of hurting the feelings of the followers of that religion could be conceived as a malicious violation of the spirit of tolerance, which was one of the bases of a democratic society' (para 15). In doing what she had done, Ms. Sabaditsch-Wolff had violated the 'religious peace in Austria' (para 15).

This concept of 'religious peace' is a recurrent theme in the comments of the Regional Austrian Court, as it was also in the Vienna Court of Appeal, which confirmed the applicant's conviction. The Vienna Court added another argument to dismiss Sabaditsch-Wolff's pedophilia accusation: Mohammed's first wife had been 15 years older than he was.

The Austrian courts convicted the accused under two articles in the Austrian Penal Code. First, Article 188, which criminalizes offenses against the religious peace (*Strafbare Handlungen gegen den religiösen Frieden*). It reads as follows:

> Whoever, in circumstances where his or her behaviour is likely to arouse justified indignation, publicly disparages or insults a person who, or an object which, is an object of veneration of a church or religious community established within the country, or a dogma, a lawful custom or a lawful institution of such a church or religious community, shall be liable to up to six months' imprisonment or a day-fine for a period of up to 360 days (para 24).

The second article is Section 283 of the Austrian Penal Code, which penalizes incitement to hatred:

> 1. Whoever, in a manner capable of endangering public order, publicly incites to commit a hostile act against a church or religious community established within the country or against a group defined by its belonging to such a church or religious community, a race, a nation, a tribe or a state, shall be liable to up to two years' imprisonment.
>
> 2. Similarly, whoever publicly incites against a group defined in paragraph 1 or tries to insult or disparage them in a manner violating human dignity shall equally be held liable (para 24).

The European Court did not reject the verdicts of the Austrian courts. The Court agreed that Sabaditsch-Wolff 'must have been aware that her statements were partly based on untrue facts and apt to arouse (justified) indignation in others' (para 54). Apparently, the Court focused on the 'untrue fact' of pedophilia while remaining silent on the age difference between Aisha and the middle-aged Prophet. There is also no further analysis in the judgment of the European Court about the right definition of pedophilia. Is it right to assume, as both the Austrian courts and the European Court do, that someone is not a pedophile if he or she *also* has sexual relationships with adults? Or is not a pedophile if he or she had a relationship with an adult later in life? Or that the pedophile label no longer applies once an underaged girl reaches the age of maturity?

The essence of Sabaditsch-Wolff's complaints seems to be the age difference between the religious icon and the underaged girl and the social consequences of that fact. This age difference is not an 'untrue fact', or at least it is not contested in Islamic lore.

A somewhat uncomfortable conclusion that may be drawn from the European Court's stance in this matter is that, at a time when certain elements of Islamic culture are in need of criticism, this criticism is stifled not only by theoterrorist attacks (Danish cartoons, French cartoons, American cartoons) (*see also* Cliteur and Herrenberg, 2016: pp. 137–157; Herrenberg, 2015: pp. 1–19) but also by judgments from the very same institutions invented to protect the freedom to criticize in 47 European countries.

Bibliography

Abdel-Samad, H (2009) *Mein Abschied vom Himmel: Aus dem Leben eines Muslims in Deutschland*, Knaur Taschenbuch Verlag, München.

Abdel-Samad, H (2010) *Der Untergang der islamischen Welt: Eine Prognose*, Droemer Verlag, München.

Abdel-Samad, H (2011) *Krieg oder Frieden: die Arabische Revolution und die Zukunft des Westens*, Droemer Verlag, München.

Abdel-Samad, H (2015) *Mohamed: Eine Abrechnung*, Droemer Verlag, München.

Abdel-Samad, H (2016) *Islamic Fascism*, Prometheus Books, Amherst, New York.

Albright, M (2018) *Fascism: A Warning*, HarperCollins Publishers, London.

Arib, K (2017) "We zijn te lang onverschillig geweest," Abel Herzberglezing, in Trouw.

Armstrong, K (1999) *A History of God: From Abraham to the Present: the 4000-Year Quest for God*, Vintage books, London (1993).

Bawer, B (2006) *While Europe Slept: How Radical Islam Is Destroying the West from Within*, Doubleday, New York, Auckland.

Ben Jelloun, T (2012) *L'islam expliqué aux enfants (et à leurs parents)*, Nouvelle édition augmentée, Éditions du Seuil, Paris (2002).

Bennoune, K (2002) "A Disease Masquarading as a Cure: Women and Fundamentalism in Algeria. An Interview with Mahfoud Bennoune," in Betsy Reed, ed., *Nothing Sacred: Women Respond to Religious Fundamentalism and Terror*, Introduction by Katha Pollitt, Thunder's Mouth Press/Nation Books, New York.

Bennoune, K (2009) "Remembering the Other's Others: Theorizing the Approach of International Law to Muslim Fundamentalism," in *Columbia Human Rights Review*, Vol. 41.

Bennoune, K (2013) *Your Fatwa Does Not Apply Here: Untold Stories from the Fight against Muslim Fundamentalism*, W.W. Norton & Company, New York, London.

Burke, J (2003) *Al-Qaeda: The True Story of Radical Islam*, Penguin Books, London.

Cliteur, P (2011) "Female Critics of Islamism," in *Feminist Theology*, 19(2).

Cliteur, P (2015) "Is Humanism Too Optimistic? An Analysis of Religion as Religion," in Andrew Copson and A.C. Grayling, eds., *The Wiley Blackwell Handbook of Humanism*, Wiley Blackwell, Chicester 2015.

Cliteur, P and Herrenberg, T (2016) "Rushdie's Critics", in: Paul Cliteur and Tom Herrenberg, eds., *The Fall and Rise of Blasphemy Law,* Leiden University Press, Leiden.

Cliteur, P and Guiora, AN (2019) *Populist and Islamist Challenges for International Law,* American Bar Association, Chicago.

Cox, C and Marks, J (2003) *The West, Islam and Islamism: Is Ideological Islam Compatible with Liberal Democracy?*, Civitas, Institute for the Study of Civil Society, London.

Delcambre, A (2003) *L'Islam des Interdits,* Desclée de Brouwer, Paris.

Delcambre, A (2004) *L'Islam,* La Découverte, Paris.

Delcambre, A (2006) *La Schizophrénie de l'Islam,* Desclée de Brouwer, Paris.

Delcambre, A (2009) *Mahomet: La parole d'Allah,* Éditions Gallimard, Paris.

Desai, M (2007) *Rethinking Islamism: The Ideology of the New Terror,* L.B. Taurus, London/New York, preface.

E.S. v. Austria, (App. 38450/12), 25 October 2018.

Esposito, JL and Mogahed, D (2007) *Who Speaks for Islam? What a Billion Muslims Really Think,* Gallup Press.

Ellian, A (2008) "Monotheism as a Political Problem: Political Islam and the Attack on Religious Equality and Freedom," in *Telos* 145 (Winter).

Euben, R (1997) "Comparative Political Theory: An Islamic Fundamentalist Critique of Rationalism," in *The Journal of Politics*, Vol. 59, No. 1 (Feb.).

Gabriel, B (2008) *They Must Be Stopped: Why We Must Defeat Radical Islam and How We Can Do It*, St. Martin's Press, New York.

Gardner, M (1996) "Beyond Cultural Relativism," in Martin Gardner, *The Night Is Large*, Collected Essays 1938-1995, Penguin Books, London.

General Intelligence and Security Service (2004) *From Dawa to Jihad: The Various Threats from Radical Islam to the Democratic Legal Order*, The Hague, December.

Gensler, HJ (1998) "Cultural Relativism," in *Ethics*, Routledge, London & New York.

Haarscher, G (2015) *Philosophie des droits de l'homme*, Nouvelle édition revue et augmentée, Les Éditions du cerf, Paris (1993).

Harris, S and Nawaz, M (2015) *Islam and the Future of Tolerance*, Harvard University Press, Cambridge, Mass., London.

Hartmann, M (1909) *Der Islam: Geschichte, Glaube, Recht, Ein Handbuch*, Verlag von Rudolf Haupt, Leipzig.

Hartmann, M (1910) "Deutschland und der Islam," in *Der Islam: Journal of the History and Culture of the Middle East*, Volume 1, Issue 1 (Jan.).

Hasan, R (2012) "We need a 21st century Voltaire to fight the growing power of censorship around the world", in: *The Independent,* 23 October.

Hasan, R (2019) "Runnymede Trust's Report on Islamophobia, 1997", in: Emma Webb, ed., *Islamophobia: An Anthology of Concerns,* Civitas, London.

Herrenberg, T (2015) "Denouncing Divinity: Blasphemy, Human Rights, and the Struggle of Political Leaders to defend Freedom of Speech in the Case of *Innocence of Muslims*", in: *Ancilla Iuris,* 1.

Hirsi Ali, A (2017) *The Challenge of Dawa: Political Islam as Ideology and Movement and How to Counter It,* Hoover Institution Press.

Husain, E (2007) *The Islamist: Why I Joined Radical Islam in Britain, What I Saw Inside and Why I Left,* Penguin Books, London.

Jansen, JJG (1997) *The Dual Nature of Islamic Fundamentalism,* Cornell University Press, Ithaca, New York.

Kepel, G (2004) *Jihad: The Trial of Political Islam,* Revised Edition, Translated by Anthony F. Roberts, I.B. Taurus, London, New York (2002).

Kilmeade, B and Yeager, D (2015) *Thomas Jefferson and the Tripoli Pirates,* Sentinel, New York.

Koopmans, R (2013) "Religious Fundamentalism and Out-Group Hostility among Muslims and Christians in Western Europe," in WZB Mitteilungen, Berlin Social Science Center, December.

Linnemann, C, Bausback, W, hg. (2019) *Der Politische Islam gehört nicht zu Deutschland*, Herder, Freiburg, Basel, Wien.

Loewenstein, K (1937a) "Militant Democracy and Fundamental Rights", I, in: *The American Political Science Review,* Vol. 31, No. 3 (June).

Loewenstein, K (1937b) "Militant Democracy and Fundamental Rights", II, in: *The American Political Science Review,* Vol 31, No. 4 (August).

Manea, E (2018) *Der alltägliche Islamismus: Terror beginnt, wo wir ihn zulassen*, Kösel Verlag, München.

Marshall, P, ed. (2005) *Radical Islam's Rules: The Worldwide Spread of Extreme Shari'a Law*, Rowman & Littlefield Publishers, Inc., Lanham etc.

Minow, M (2007) "Tolerance in an Age of Terror," in: *Southern California Interdisciplinary Law Journal*, Vol. 16.

Moller Okin, S (1999) *Is Multiculturalism Bad for Women?*, with Respondents, edited by Joshua Cohen, Matthew Howard, and Martha Nussbaum, Princeton University Press, Princeton, New Jersey.

Murray, T (2018) *Identity, Islam and the Twilight of Liberal Values*, Cambridge Scholars Publishing, Cambridge.

Najjar, FM (1998) "Islamic Fundamentalism and the Intellectuals: The Case of Naguib Mahfouz," in *British Journal of Middle Eastern Studies*, Vol. 25, No. 1 (May).

Obama, B (2009) "Speech in Cairo," June 4, 2009, in *The New York Times*, June 4.

Osman, T (2016) *Islamism: What it means for the Middle East and the World*, Yale University Press, New Haven and London.

Pierik, P (2015) *Islamitische Staat: Achtergronden—(broeder)strijd—helden en beulengeopolitieke consequenties*, Aspekt, Soesterberg.

Pipes, D (2002) *Militant Islam Reaches America*, W.W. Norton & Company, New York, London.

Pipes, D (2005) *In the Path of God: Islam and Political Power*, with a new preface by the author, Transaction Publishers, New Brunswick and London (2002).

Prothero, S (2010) *God Is Not One: The Eight Rival Religions That Run the World*, HarperOne, New York.

Ramadani, Z (2017) *Die verschleierte Gefahr: die Macht der muslimischen und der Toleranzwahn der Deutschen*, Europa Verlag, München.

Rijpkema, B (2018) *Militant Democracy*, Routledge, London and New York.

Rizvi, AA (2016) *The Atheist Muslim: A Journey from Religion to Reason*, St. Martin's Press, New York.

Sajó, A (2004) *Militant Democracy,* Eleven, International Publishing, Utrecht.

Samuelson, K (2017) "Read Prime Minister Theresa May's Full Speech on the London S Bridge Attack," in *Time World,* June 4.

Sansal, B (2013) *Gouverner au nom d'Allah: Islamisation et soif de pouvoir dans le monde arabe,* Gallimard, Paris.

Schmidt-Salomon, M (2016) *Die Grenzen der Toleranz: Warum wir die offene Gesellschaft verteidigen müssen,* Piper, München, Berlin, Zürich.

Schröter, S (2019) *Politischer Islam: Stresstest für Deutschland,* Gütersloher Verlagshaus, Gütershoh.

Schwabach, A (2010) "Thomas Jefferson, Slavery, and Slaves," in 33 *T. Jefferson L. Rev.,* 1.

Schwarzer, A Hrsg. (2010) *Die Große Verschleierung: für Integration, gegen Islamismus,* Kiepenheuer & Witsch, Köln, p. 14.

Spencer, R (2002) *Islam Unveiled: Disturbing Questions about the World's Fastest-Growing Faith,* Encounter Books, San Francisco.

Spencer, R (2012) *Did Mohammad Exist? An Inquiry into Islam's Obscure Origins,* Wilmington, Delaware.

Spencer, R (2015) *The Complete Infidel's Guide to ISIS,* Regnery Publishing, Washington.

Taguieff, P (2017) *L'islamisme et nous. Penser l'ennemi imprévu*, CNRS Éditions, Paris.

Tibi, B (2008) *Political Islam, World Politics and Europe: Democratic Peace and Euro-Islam versus Global Jihad*, Routledge, London and New York.

Tibi, B (2001) *Europa ohne Identität? Leitkultur oder Wertebeliebigkeit*, 2e Auflage, Siedler, München (1998).

Tibi, B (2012) *Islamism and Islam*, Yale University Press, New Haven and London.

Tibi, B (2013) *The Sharia State: Arab Spring and Democratization*, Routledge, London and New York.

Tibi, B (2019a) "Dankesrede: I'll state my case, of which I'm certain: I did it my way: Leidener Unbequeme Gedanken", in: Bassam Tibi, *Basler Unbequeme Gedanken über illegale Zuwanderung, Islamisierung und Unterdrückung der Redefreiheit*, Aktualisiert, überarbeitet, erweitert, mit einem Geleitwort von Benedict Neff, Ibidem-Verlag, Stuttgart.

Tibi, B (2019b) "Introduction", in: Paul Cliteur, *Theoterrorism v. Freedom of Speech,* Amsterdam University Press, Amsterdam.

Trump, D (2016) "Donald Trump's Speech on Fighting Terrorism," Republican candidate Donald Trump, speech delivered in Youngstown, Ohio, August 15, 2016 in *Politico*, August 15.

Trump, D (2017) "Address in Saudi Arabia," May 21, in thehill.com.

Van den Bergh, G (2019) "The Democratic State and the Non-Democratic Parties", in: Paul Cliteur and Amos N. Guiora, *Populist and Islamist Challenges for International Law*, American Bar Association, Chicago.

Zee, M (2014) "Five Options for the Relationship between the State and Sharia Councils," in *Journal of Religion and Society*, Volume 16.

Zee, M (2015) *Choosing Sharia: Multiculturalism, Islamic Fundamentalism & British Sharia Councils*, Eleven, The Hague.

Zuckerman, P and Shook, J, eds. (2017) *The Oxford Handbook of Secularism*, Oxford Handbooks, Oxford/New York.

Biography

Paul Cliteur (1955) is a professor of jurisprudence, connected to the department of jurisprudence at Leiden University. He was also a professor of philosophy at the University of Delft (1995-2002); visiting professor at Hastings College of the Law in California (2017); and the University of Ghent (2014).

He wrote/edited about 40 books, including *Theoterrorism versus Freedom of Speech* (2019), *A New Introduction to Legal Method* (2022), *A New Introduction to Jurisprudence* (2019), *Populist and Islamist Challenges for International Law* (2019), *Bardot, Fallaci, Houellebecq and Wilders* (2016).

He contributed to the *Oxford Handbook of Secularism* (2017) and the *Wiley-Blackwell Handbook of Humanism* (2015) and wrote op-eds for *The Finland Times, The New York Times, Reformatorisch Dagblad, NRC,* De *Volkskrant, Trouw, Het Parool, HP/De Tijd, Vrij Nederland, The PostOnline,* and *De Dagelijkse Standaard.*

He supervised about 25 Ph.D. students in writing their dissertations. He is now working on translating his book *The Secular Outlook* (2010) into Dutch as *The Secular Vision* (2022).

www.ingramcontent.com/pod-product-compliance
Lightning Source LLC
Chambersburg PA
CBHW050541270326
41926CB00015B/3333